Story by Carmel Reilly

Illustrations by Sarah Davis

## Contents

## Chapter 1

# A New Friend

It was lunchtime at Highbury School.
Josh grabbed a ball and raced outside.
As he ran onto the football field, he saw Ben.
Ben was new at school. He had just started that week.

"Do you want to play football with me?" Josh asked Ben.

"That would be great," said Ben.

Josh booted the ball towards Ben.
Ben caught it and kicked it into the goal.

"You're really good!" said Josh.

"Thanks," said Ben.

Ben and Josh practised their goal kicking until the bell rang. Then, they walked together back to their classroom.

"Would you like to come over to my place on Saturday?" Ben asked Josh. "We have a huge backyard. There's lots of space to kick a ball around."

"That would be great," said Josh. "I can't play football at my place. Our backyard is too small."

Chapter 2

# Something Better

As Josh was leaving school the next day,
he saw his friend, Ethan.

"Do you want to come bowling on Saturday?"
Ethan asked Josh.
"We are going to get pizza when we finish."

"I would really like to go bowling," said Josh.
"But I've made plans to go to Ben's house."

"No, you should come with me!" said Ethan.
"You'll have much more fun.
You can go to Ben's place another time."

Josh knew that it would be fun to go bowling with Ethan.

When Josh got home later that afternoon, he told his mother he wanted to go out with Ethan on Saturday.

"But is that the right thing to do?" asked Mum. "You told Ben that you would go to his place, didn't you?"

Josh thought for a little while.
"Yes, I did," he said, at last.
"And I should keep my word, shouldn't I?"

"Well, Josh, you will know what to do," said Mum.

## Chapter 3

# Saturday Morning

On Saturday morning, Mum took Josh to Ben's place. After talking to Ben's dad for a few minutes, Mum said goodbye to Josh.

"I think you are going to have a great time here," she said.

Josh nodded, but he couldn't stop thinking about the fun he could be having with Ethan.
He didn't really want to be at Ben's today.

After Mum left, Josh and Ben went outside and kicked the football around the backyard.

The morning passed quickly, and Josh was surprised when Ben's dad called them in for lunch.

"Your mum said you like going to the movies," said Ben's dad.

Josh smiled. “I really like action movies,” he said.

“So do I!” said Ben.

“Well, let’s go and see one this afternoon,” said Ben’s dad.

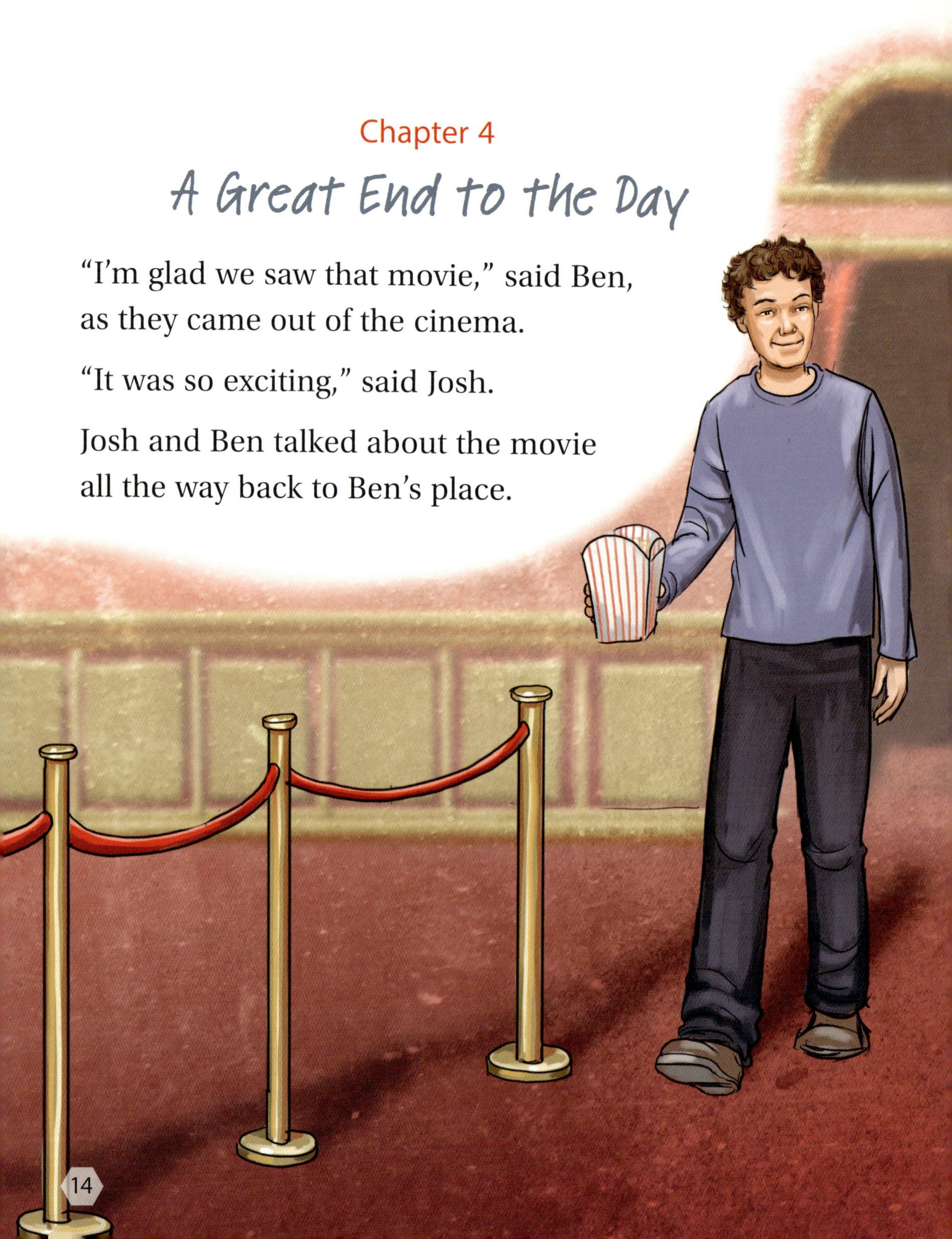

Chapter 4

# A Great End to the Day

"I'm glad we saw that movie," said Ben, as they came out of the cinema.

"It was so exciting," said Josh.

Josh and Ben talked about the movie all the way back to Ben's place.

They were still talking about it when Josh's mum arrived to pick him up.

"I've had a really great day," Josh said to Ben, as he left.

"It sounds like you had a good time after all, Josh," Mum said, as they walked home.

Josh smiled. "I'm so glad that I kept my word," he said. "I had an amazing day – and I've made a new friend."